Be Feared

Be Feared

Jane Burn

Nine
Arches
Press

Be Feared
Jane Burn

ISBN: 978-1-913437-27-5
eISBN: 978-1-913437-28-2

Copyright © Jane Burn, 2021

Cover artwork: 'Be Feared' © Jane Burn

All rights reserved. No part of this work may be reproduced, stored or transmitted in any form or by any means, graphic, electronic, recorded or mechanical, without the prior written permission of the publisher.

Jane Burn has asserted her right under Section 77 of the Copyright, Designs and Patents Act 1988 to be identified as the author of this work.

First published November 2021 by:

Nine Arches Press
Unit 14, Sir Frank Whittle Business Centre,
Great Central Way, Rugby.
CV21 3XH
United Kingdom

www.ninearchespress.com

Nine Arches Press is supported using public funding by Arts Council England.

To Lindsay,

for helping to make one of my biggest dreams come true.

Contents

Trepanation	11
Coronach for my slender waist	13
Mrs/Mother Hail	15
How Austistic Spectrum Condition Made Her Worth Her Weight in Birds	17
The Only Kind of Poetry I Seem to be Able to Write	18
Triolet for Easter and the icon I have made of a wizened rabbit's pelt	19
Look at me, lingering outside this murdered church	20
Self-Portrait as an Inferno	21
Thumbelina's Birth as Told in the Style of Gregorian chant	22
So you made a thousand shit decisions	23
Fairy Stories	24
Fat Alice	25
This is a Frankenstein Night	26
Schneewittchen and the Universe	27
Aubade to the Noise of Chainsaws	28
Red	29
Aubade to a Wedding Photograph	30
Gerda's searching leads her to roses and, at the edge of the Snow Queen's land, she realises that her Autism will always be the fairytale with no satisfactory end	31
The Cursing Psalm	36
Hood	37
There are things that give me away if you know how to look,	38
Frances Cornford's poem about a lady in gloves makes me realise that I have feelings for a woman for the first time	39
The nights in which I fantasise an evensong of us	40
Are Vaginas a Deal-Breaker Thing?	41
We could live in a cwtch of castles. I'll grow my hair	42
The First Time I Really, Properly Swim	43
I was not the eye of the Hubble. I saw no cosmic string	44
Villanelle to Cold Psalms	45

Quiero saber si tú aun me quieres and imagining seeing a bird burning in the sky	46
Study of Life as Recorded in Cruel Lines	48
Grin Both Ways	49
The love that Orca taught me while he grew	50
Ode to the Sight of my Coloured Cob	52
The gifts she got at birth	53
Poor blackbird crumb	54
Be subtle as the Snow Queen,	55
The truth began with a mirror, clean and cruel	56
Magic Mirror	57
My Offering to the Earth	58
November's Spoil of Rain and Plague	59
Ways in which I came to be a thief	60
The Altar of the Dead	61
Spun from the Same	62
The Un-Flight of Porcelain Birds	63
How the river takes whatever you pray	64
If we are here when yellow has done with the year	65
Is Autism/COVID happening to someone/somewhere else?	66
The Advent Calendar of Most Useful Things	67
Spun from the Same	68
If Ω Is For The Last Thing I Might Ever Do	69
Acknowledgements	71

Trepanation

Or what my life became when I let the ghouls out of my brain

Once I thought I knew   the way of fields
I thought that I had seen   the view's only truth
I spread upon   the tender world of moss

yielded my head   to the ground
gave passage   to any questing root
my mind an offering   to pullulations of seed

the auger's turn unwound   the true smell of grass
the bitter beauty of   the sapid green
my cerebrum devoured   the piquancy of growing corn

a chalice to bear   the piety of freshly fallen rain
silver-sharp against   the path of my own rushing veins
its ions broke upon   the scaffold of my bones

I opened my head to   the luminous fusion of stars
let myself wear   the incredible weight of night
filled my skull with   the raw coin of the moon

felt its halo bloom inside   my own cavern of bone
I woke beneath   my version of a morning sky
the wound uncumbered   my devout kaleidoscope

my pate throbbed with welts   of immense blue
I drilled myself aware   of great definitions of cloud
uncovered a world   of high-borne froth

the universe inside   each airborne fleck of ice
their unmapped journey across   each astonishing vault
I thought I knew the whole sound of   each bird

such new complexities from   the delicious well of their throats
such patterns to describe   the shape of flight
I saw each barbule hold   the whole wing against the wind

I could not taste   the ghosts that I had kept
I could not hoard   the wandered voice of distal pain
I could not recall   the ubiquity of your face

How Austistic Spectrum Condition
Made Her Worth Her Weight in Birds

Pitter-scratch, patter-scratch, soil-deluded beak.
The floor is a mystery of worms, a concealment of seeds.
This queerish bird keeps becoming lost, though she is not a tiny thing.

See how this bird knocks her cheek against a cupboard door
and *bat, bat, bat!* comes a sound of wood bumping against flesh.
The smell of varnish, bitter. The nurture of wood, divine.

Elbow-flicker, elbow-flack, great misguided flight. The air
is a flabbergast of space, a fatigue of liberty. An unreachable scar.
She sees it marked by a devotion of swans and worships

their berth, the lowering of fat unblemished bows. Their christening
of self to shifting water, their mustering of signets into lines.
She is afraid she does not lead her own baby well,

afraid he will drown in her chaos. She is all the horrors
of doing things wrong though she lowers her neck above him
in shapes of love. What sort of bird might she be?

Not the harsh slice of gulls – she did not abandon her chick
to sheer cliff, would never risk his un-flight fall, nor his mite's casting
to jaws of rock. How she fluffs around this treasure!

Waggle-squat, scuffle-crouch, bulk resigned frame.
The floor's moor is a complex of heather, peeps of mottled plume.
This bird is folding upon a stool's perch. Look how she has laid

the addled shell of her head to the length of the table's slab.
This bird has ways of guessing wind though she is not a free thing
and *press, press, press,* comes lush, dull pain, a blissful blank,

a bright nest in her brow. She muses upon the plunge of cormorants.
Needles, stitching themselves to fathoms of salt. Oceans
have no corners – is the sea is too big a space?

Reflections were never her friend. She spurs at the wrong-ways
repeating of herself. No matter how she swims, there will be no split
from this clinging twin – the drag of her aping curse.

Gravel-gullet, splinter-hymn, rasp of ugly verse. Compline
is nightmare time, a tuneless ask. She is no nightingale – her voice
of shatter and shriek chimes for every hour that she forces

her breast to thorns. One this weight will never hum for nectar,
no matter how she puts tongue to bloom. She envies the swallows,
prays for such frail connects. *Quop-fleck, dash-fear,* spook

from human sight. The day is a threat of lungs, a worry of sounds.
She harbours aspects of a wren, as *pit, pit, pit,* she weaves
a home of threads. *Picky-snap, scrabble-snap,* her hands

are clacking bills, plucking her purse of screwed receipts, pecking
at paper scat. This bird winds herself with spells as *bind, bind, bind,*
she is lured back to ground. Becomes concious of blood.

This bird was born a murmuration. From inside her mouth
comes a flight, a flurry for this is the way she cries. Catch them,
though they are not perceptible things and *flit, flit, flit,*

there are hollows in her chest. This bird is built on bruised
and brittle sticks. Look how she carries a craw of knives that cut
through all her songs. Though she will say *I'm fine, I'm fine,*

there is no cure for cracks. The tap drips its chorus through dawn.
This bird has a secret, caught behind her lips. Look how her tongue
toils like a trapped wing. It will spiel feathers and *sing, sing, sing*

a question of sky. Her kitchen is an aviary. She sees blue, its colour
served through cracks. Who made her mocking brain?
Sometimes it is an eyrie, scribbled with scraps and full of bones.

She is an owl's breaking of dusk, the steeple of an egret.
Dot-dash, dot-dash, her toes cling to ledges like walking code.
She writes a riddle with each step. *Home, Sweet Home, Sweet Home.*

The Only Kind of Poetry I Seem to be Able to Write
After 'The Kind of Poetry I Want' by Hugh MacDiarmid

And so I must consider the time I was almost fish –
when life was blood and water, when sound came to me
through bone and scales and meat. I knew my mother as a tun
and there I grew from tiny round, translucent shrimp, to nix.
I drank. I swam and flickered, pissed and kicked. Was a miracle
for a while. How happy is a body that does not know?
I clung to her warm bank like a glass eel.
My head built a creel of esoteric wires.

And so I must yield to the months of peculiar thirst.
I dreamed the smell of freshly gathered grain and made
an angel of its golden dust, knelt before my pica need
for good soil, put my nose to earthy tempt and closed
the craving shovel of my mouth. I prayed to be
the perfect mum and if not that, allow my love to be
a natural thing – a bird, a tree, a dusk-delicious moth.
Make me good and strong around my child.

And so I must discover how deep to wound,
how much of my own heart to yield to the blade.
How much of myself must I bleed across the page?
Must I build a poem from lines of squandered love
and hang myself from its frame? This is the only reason
I wanted you, in the end – so my words could follow
the shape of scars, so the last verse I write could be
a chrysalis of pain.

And so I must consider my own habits – how I feel
summer is not complete without sweet alyssum, its intoxicate
of fragrant snow. Not complete without the planting of seeds,
the pressing of their germ below a lip of soil,
the birth of frail green spires. They will bloom
and I will skim their scent from the surface of the day.
The rest of life is ruin. I have lost control
of everything but them.

And so I must drowse, a ponyskin of shadow and light,
wake and yawn like a cracked egg.
As the sun fails beneath a milk of afternoon mist
I rouse to see a centipede of flying geese –
walk to where I can learn from the sacrifice of small things –
blossom's shortened beauty, its willing waste.
I see blunt and coppiced trees, the dense pelts
of moss making a universe on their wounds.

Coronach for my slender waist

Pardon me my weight.
I wrapped your spindle with pain.
Once, I could button up around you tight.
Once I did not have to purchase clothes with space enough
to hood my fat cathedral.
The paper eats my shame.

Once written, a word becomes a garden.
The paper is a field and you have set words free.
The paper is a tablet and you have set words in stone.
You have emptied yourself.
You have filled yourself again.
You learned the rapture of overindulgence,

the agony of a blunted pen.
The word is an iron nail,
the invasion of myself into beautiful space.
I want the paper to feel the impression of my head.
The paper is true to my bones.
Once written, a word leaves its comfort on your tongue,

leaves its boot against your brain.
I am the mortal fear of mirrors.
I have the throat of a passerine,
the stomach of a whale.
My shadow is a mountain.
The paper takes my stains.

Mrs/Mother   Hail

Mrs/Mother   blessed art the windowpanes
    O keep us from the lure of dust
      forgive this   hankering for distant lanes
    give us   brave   archangels of morning sun

Mrs/Mother   hail the dull bulb of scratched spoons
    for we must lift the humility of soup
      O   deliver us from   the sin of bread
    excuse the rough palm   its trespassing of skin

Mrs/Mother   O let us learn the hollow curse of curdled pans
    the evil   celibacy of the washing up
      the everlasting   weight of a dowager's hump
    lead us not   into the drowning of knives

Mrs/Mother   O   pity thy uncovered fruit
    pray for the sake of   one small brown bruise
      for the baptism   of potatoes   for the hour
    of their laying bare   the mining of sprouted eyes

Mrs/Mother   O   speak as one who stoops to crumbs
    glory! for the cumber of a used womb
      have mercy upon the   quiet chapel of upturned cups
    suffer the bowl's foam   the smell of grass

Mrs/Mother   O   rise before such nights of bleak glass
    light without end   and   light and   light and   light!
      and forever there shall be   the sight of birds
    invisible tastes of water   amen

Triolet for Easter and the icon I have made of a wizened rabbit's pelt

This journey round your folded bones, your mess of meagre limbs
becomes a necessary crusade. Each day, I must repair your psalter of wounds –

rotate you so that each eye has equal sight of the sky's smalt scrim.
This journey round your folded bones, your mess of meagre limbs

ends with my kneeling at your reliquary of grass. The parchment of your skin
waits like a page, to be written with colours of God. Once, blood bloomed

and made its journey round your folded bones. Your mess of meagre limbs
becomes a necessary crusade, each day. I must repair your psalter of wounds.

Look at me, lingering outside this murdered church

Open your lids, you coal-smut, bitter thing. Undraw the blind
that plunged doom has set in the lead of your eyes.
Too many years of chimneys, licking filth on your bricks.
Nobody comes to pluck at your weeds. Look at the pair of us,
our caverns unused. Methodists didn't build for beauty –
face like a mortuary slab, barren grim of harsh white walls,
let me in and I'll sing you some saints. God, for me, has not
been enough. If I am to believe, daub me some vivid grief,
gouge this wasted cave with a burning of Sacred Hearts.
I will treat this bare render with my own crude litter of faith.
You were laboured, foundations up by your devout, by the skill
of pious flesh – they met and worshipped, passed
the plain, small wealth of a humble plate. Against your shell,
I hear the memory of Sunday School, feel the holy flattening
of my arse after hours pressed to the hard wood seat,
colouring the lines of Gentle Jesus, playing with
the brittle thin of simple, twisted palm. Thus we were made
by a plain religion. I craved the gibber of rosaries, the veils,
the fondant of Communion gowns, the thurible swinging
fumes of dedication up. The wailing visions of Virgin's smalt,
tabernacles, the myth of Saviour's blood. My prayers
will splatter your crypt with messy devotions.
My hymns are huge. I am an exorcism. Am here to spew
devils at your altar's feet, did not expect to find
the slam and hasp of ailing Gothic doors. I make
what I think is the requisite sign, poking my relic of belly
and tits. An empty cross to show that I already suffered and won.
Open up, you barred and bolted thing.

Self-Portrait as an Inferno

I saw the birth of a crazy phoenix – saw it raise hackles of fire,
span bright wings of pain, sear the night with a flock of sparks.

It made a spear of embers and flew its pyre into the dusk –
crackled with vicious feathers, spat its language of loss

from an orange tongue. I looked it square in its red-cleft beak,
saw a gizzard drunk with boiling doom, saw it arm the flue

of its neck with bellyfuls of apocalypse. This blistered bird
pegged talons to my cheeks and infiltrated every breath

with filth. *I've had uglier meat than you down my scalded throat,*
I crowed and beat my voice against the smouldered void.

My pupils rolled wide as dark wheels – I wore the shape of flames
upon my eyes, doused tinder beneath each blink, met its furnace

and found that I was not afraid. *I've been through worse,* I hissed
into its scorching ear, then watered vessels full and bore it a cure

of moon-bucket pools to quench its rage, wore its shroud
of vengeful smoke like my own defiant coat. I cursed it in its own

kindle speech. Grew hooded with dust, tasted reeking air
and lapped the dry well of my parched mouth, looked toward

my aftermath of sooty hair and frowned the colour of fumes.
I saw the mark of evil flight upon my skin, was alive though

the night had flickered with angels, made a cinder of my face.
I was an echo of waste, built from tomorrow's cold remains.

Thumbelina's Birth as Told in the Style of Gregorian chant

I grew in the furl of a flower's heart,
its quilted walls licked round me like fragrant tongues. Suckled on syrup,

I bloomed my puck of a body, sprouted
each stem of my tiny limbs. My birth was nectar, each pistil holding me

spindle-tight. I was consummated gold – pollen
blessing my newborn bones. Above the posy's scoop a woman loomed,

ten thousand times my size – my mother,
who prayed for a spark to kindle-full her dormant womb and I was the rapture

that burst from a bud. She polished
a half-shell for my bed, spilled a beauty of lullabies over my walnut crib.

I slept for I did not know, back then
that a toad would leer through a broken pane of glass – that I would wake

in the covet of knobbled arms, that I'd
wear the clutch of a chafer at my waist, that nights would fear a thrumming

song. That winter would come, and stubble
rise to cut the thin of my skin with blades. That I'd come to dread the smother

of moles – the looming plush of their
velvet cloaks, the dots of dark in their eyes. That I would cry for the sight

of a fallen bird and weave his pity a pelt
of hay, that he would bear my weight upon his hollow bones, that I would

think of the freedom I held between
my legs. Of the swallow who was my love.

So you made a thousand shit decisions

Forgive yourself, you poor wreck Remember when he used to say
I'll find you I'll follow you   Everything you do or say,
I'll know I have my ways   of finding out.

Remeber when you stayed numb as a block   with his hands
around your neck   how you made a fixation of the ceiling above
safe in swirls of Artex   How he claimed your acquiescence

for a yes   how it looked just like you didn't feel a thing
like his stony bulb of cock was pushing its way into the soft
of someone else

You had nothing to compare him with   What a baptism!
When you felt him in you   you cried   when you kicked your legs
it was too late and you   he said   had been   *broken in*

Forgive yourself   you shambles   You had the mind
of a child still   His cum stank like dead air
You wore a font of blood   It stung

Fairy Stories

I am Rapunzel in her tower with her hair already shorn,
or Sleeping Beauty, pricked not by a spinning needle
but by some more poisonous thorn.

I am Cinderella, but my slippers are not glass –
they are rusted iron shackles locked
so tight no key can pass.

I am Snow White but now, instead of tasting purest skin,
I am spat bites of bad apple,
stained both outside and in.

I am the Little Mermaid – I walk on spikes of pain.
The ocean's crested waves
will never salve my scales again.

I am the faded Goose Girl – my charms have slowly paled.
I am stripped of my silk dancing dresses
while my Falada hangs from a nail.

Alas, he could not teach to me the things I never knew.
I must tell my truths to cast iron doors
and my heart will break in two.

Fat Alice

put her foot in a rabbit hole, fell like a sack of spuds,
almost set her neck. *Curious*, she says,

cheek on the grass, ankle shrieking, knee dunched,
neck lashed. *Curious that nothing*

broke my fall. She spits dust, face bloomed
with humiliation, jam tart red. Her arms brace.

Each hand, bent at the wrists makes the shape of a flamingo –
she might stand and make a giant. Might lay,

sickle on the deck like a Cheshire smile
some passing mouth cast off. The sky is smooth

as mushrooms, her shadow a *drink-this* tisane's skin.
Fat Alice all doddering, bone-sore and limping goes back

to her house of cards. There's a table waiting,
filthed with gorge and crumb, one used teabag

slumped in a cup like a mouse on drugs. Fat Alice
scrumples her To-Do list. It was filled with impossible

things. There is pain in the caterpillar of her spine.
She is going to be late for everything.

This is a Frankenstein Night

Rebuild the monsters in your life. Finish work in the dark, pace
the salted car park to where you parked. You spent the shift
smiling, cramping on un-passed wind. The waistband bites.
Check behind, let go of painful blusters as you waggle across
the stiffened grit. Turn to unlock the car. Be feared that someone
might grab your back, pull out your lungs, crack your spine,
ground you like a broken doll. Sit at the wheel and scream
your breath. Press a thumbnail to the opposite hand and scrape

a beautiful traipse of pain. Mourn the lack of spectacle. Too much
night for birds. Snatch what you can from the headlight's fan.

Stretch your voice to the radio. Make your throat a wishing well.

Schneewittchen and the Universe

Gaia, peeling its orbit, purling apple-round, tempts her to sleep,
land her giant's head, seek nestle space in poison combs of forest.
She finds it easier to stand, big legs bracing the clouds

softly floating at her crotch. She remembers the first time –
gusset a cotton breezeblock, the feeling of learning to walk, over again.
Tucked precious with her secret and afraid of stains –

Snow White, Rose Red – she foots the lithosphere and mountains
crumb beneath her heels. She wonders at her hugeness.
Must be all this sun and rain, this good moist ground.

Dredging the ozone through her lungs, she is fat on gobbled light.
See me run! The oceans turn puddle against her wading shins – her spatters
hit the sea, congeal in the air, make land. *I have bled you islands!*

Her bits of fallen womb are worlds not born from the plots of man,
with their minds of steel and atom bombs. *Bone of my bones,
flesh of my flesh!* There is nothing here that was not brought

in a woman's blood. She lies in the cool of icebergs, large
in the glassy coffin of the poles, crimson on frost like bear-kill,
like my own beloved mum, who dreamed a girl of soot

and pale and blushes. She makes a magic mirror of the haloes
around the moon. Pulls faces, makes a moue of berry lips. Finds stories
above. *Who is the fairest of them all?* Not Orion, the rapist

written in stars. Stolen Ganymede? The judgement of Crux?
The night's splendour is named with fear. She pokes her tongue
at the hissing pearls of Hydra, the sequin haunt of Styx.

Aubade to the Noise of Chainsaws

Let us be in denial through the passions of night.
There is weakness in me that wants you –
all these years, I ought to be cured. You make
a warmth of weight above my spread. Here
is my body's betrayal. Here is a punishment of lust.

The stranded *Durex* wizens on the floor, wears
a weirdness of krill's phosphor. Neck knotted,
its head lolls with throttled sperm. My womb pulls,
gripes an accusation that I leave it bereft. You move
and a bale of heat fumes from the pit beneath.

I'm stifled. The oxygen is used, the air stinks
of sweat, the sex we had, of fish-stale breath.
I reach beyond the dump of your slumbered form,
crack the window – with relief let in
An owl's speech, a flood of fresh cold,

the waspish grizzle of a chainsaw, hungering
its belt of teeth into trees. Someone else who cannot sleep,
who has come out to butcher and hack, rather than
pass under any more wasted hours. A car trundles by.
The day is calling birds to her waking side.

Dawn bleeds the curtain's opened wound,
carves our edges with first light.
I nudge your hillock, slowly breathing still.
Get up. Please. Get out.
There is much I am yet to forgive you for.

Red

Let the bones you have crushed rejoice, I memorise as I am bid,
for I am now good as gold. *I have learned from my mistakes,
I am good!* I cry to the closed wood of the church door.
I am humbled now, I whisper to the grasping lock.
The nails do not blink – fix me with a hundred dead-iron eyes.
I loved to dance. What in God's name was wrong with that?
I smirched the Sundays with my swirling. I saw the most
beautiful shoes. It was the colour most, I think. Poppies,
sunset, roses, cherries, each step on the path like a spot of blood.
I slipped my toes through clefts of crimson silk – waltzed
on broken hearts. They carried me on, these two tight pockets,
fitted close as gloves, span me in relentless wheels.
I saw a man with sunlight seared on the edge of his axe –
one sweep and I was severed from the giddiness of my feet.

...let the bones you have crushed rejoice from Psalm 51

Aubade to a Wedding Photograph

Just as the birds find their first voice and break the hush
of silent dawn, I turn to watch the calmness
of your still-dozed face – note how age has journeyed
upon it, sung a threnody to passing time.
Your cheek is loose, bunched where it is pillowed – pressed
fabric has left a scrunched echo in your skin.
Your eyes, crowed with lines flit beneath their flimsy
film of lid, telling a tale of dreams. Your hair
is thinner, seamed with grey. I am a mirror –
the face I turn towards you is worn and torn
the same. As we breathe, the creep of early sun
knifes the curtain's gap, balances airborne dust
upon its blade. Our ribs are creels – the hearts held

inside tender as urchins, pulsing our sleep.
I make a kind of mermaid, sitting, back propped,
legs wrapped. You make the shape of a dolphin, curved
mid-leap. On the wall, our young selves pooled in glass,
looking like kids in grown-up clothes. Frothy dress,
uptight suit – our smiles are so unblemished. Now
we are weathered as salted wood. I get up,
leave you in the shipwreck of our bed. Slipper
the cold fish of my feet, aim for the kitchen,
swim the teapot, brew a golden wash. Keening
flocks of gulls are wintering out on oceans
of plough, their cries strange upon the hollow sky.
I sense the waking waves, hear you stirring in the sheets.

Gerda's searching leads her to roses and, at the edge of the Snow Queen's land, she realises that her Autism will always be the fairytale with no satisfactory end

i.

Gerda / bright / much more than snow / than smithered glass
Gerda / brave / who travelled seven tales / seven scapes of fear

First / the mirror saw warp and spoil / saw Heaven and shed its evil skin
First / Kay thought her beautiful / fouled her in its mirrored grim

Second / knew Kay and flowers / grown aslant in septic eyes
Second / was a brittle Queen and Kay / amnesiac beneath her bitter kiss

Third / how Gerda wailed for death / how swallows told Gerda true things
Third / was an offer of red shoes / of honest rivers / of heedless bloom

Fourth / and Gerda learned *alone* / was grateful for a crow's idea of love
Fourth / was a castle and Kay / was not the right castle / not the right Kay

Fifth / met a robber-girl / fierce who slept with knives / with Gerda in her bed
Fifth / told a deer's return to the Lights / of its sweet pelt mid Gerda's legs

Sixth / was a woman with paper fish / a woman who could thread the wind
Sixth / saw Gerda's naked feet / Gerda praying angels against all bad shapes

Seventh / built a place of hollow halls / an *Eternity* wrought in codes of cold
Seventh / and Gerda thawed his spite / Kay the colour of roses again

ii.

What had the River done with Gerda's love?
If you tell me, she said, *I will give you my favourite things.*
Love is worth much more than shoes. No matter the sight

of her plain skin blooming with scarlet bows, no matter
that she caught her own glance, blush and sweet in the mirror toes.
Wearing them was like pushing her feet into two bright hearts.

Gerda saw the River's gloom and cried into its dark, suspicious fill.
She cast away the dainty pair, saw how they made curious boats –
the River nodded as if it knew, tasted this unwanted gift

and lipped it back to shore, for it had claimed no life. The River
remembered how Kay and the Queen had passed – how ice
had choked the edges of its living, flowing vein.

Gerda saw her rippled echo swim its patent skin. She saw
her drowning gaze. *Pass the comb through skeins of hair,
time and time again and forget.* She found that she could

be fooled by flowers – bliss after all those months of frost.
But why, she says. *But why are there no roses?* She must not
see roses, else she will remember him! Tiger-Lily tells her

about pyres, how everyone ends up cinders. Kay as ashes? *No.*
There is no taste of him in the flames. Convolvulus binds
and weaves, speaks in creeping ribbons of green.

There is no Kay in the buds that burst on the stems.
Hyacinths fill the moon's dish with their translucent smell.
When their petals fall, onion coffins will take them to the soil.

They had tolled a head of bells but not for Kay. Buttercup offers
a heart of sun. Kay's own is cold. He must have gone
where all love is stolen by snow and the rose who had sent

its roots into the citadel of buried bones, the rose who knew
of blood and thorns, the rose who stood against the sky
like an open wound, said *we could not taste him in the earth.*

He is not dead.

iii.

Gerda's answer came in the form of a crow / who came to her
like inkblots spilled upon the snow / half-gibbet / half widow's weed
and she clung to it / Poor Gerda, forever asking everyone / everything
have you seen / The answer was in the morgue of its throat / It spoke
in shatters / She kissed the crow upon its poky beak / tasted sharps

Are you sure / are you sure / she said for corvid-speak
is the wrong tongue for human ears / *Kay is at the castle
and his boots creak loud on ice, just like our love songs sound
Go like a tame crow and seek.*
She found a man asleep in bed / kissed the length of his neck

but it was not him / it was not him / Oh Gerda / why this searching
Gerda, just think of your journey / For you have known
what others can only conjure in their dreams / You have seen
a window that warned of winter in its frozen lake / a pair
of red shoes carried on the river like a broken heart

a forgetful gardening of bloom / the miracle of a talking crow
a castle with a roof of glass / a letter written on a slate of fish
Oh Gerda / this is a place to fear the eyes with blinding charm
with flakes that fall in the shape of bears
Gerda spoke her prayer and it flew from her mouth

like a dread angel / crept its misting feathers along the ice
She came to a castle built of a hundred halls / The walls
were snow / the windows were glaciers / and shadows dwelt
in colours of blue and mystic green
Each room was a tomb of cold

iv.

In the throne-room sat a Queen, still upon the mirror
of a frozen lake and next to her was Kay,
foolish addled fellow, indigo with cold,
left to spell out an eternity of shards.
There was a cracking sound – it was the noise
of memory breaking in the casket of his heart,
the noise of wheels, trying to turn inside his solid mind.
Gerda spoke her prayer and the wind grew mild,
lay down its quiver of blades. They cried splinters,
howled the mirror's spelk of evil out, sang till the pain
of spall and needle went.

v.

But now the Snow Queen has set her haunting loose
She says *somewhere in the world it is always winter*

Her voice is the gale that breaks upon the gable end
Her spite is a snuffed candle, curling like strange breath

She says *you and me, we do not know what love is*
Put a palm to your chest and feel the last beats of a dying bird

Consider your own vitric bones, dwell upon their marrow of ice
Gerda, close your door against a storm of broken glass

Sweep the step of a settlement of spelks
Seclude yourself behind a window's solid pond

Bathe and let floes of bubbles claim your bloated form
Wish you had the courage to drown

Bind your home with keeping spells of cold
Open your mouth and show a hail of teeth

She says *pile against the skirting board as if you are a drift*
Crawl the tundra of the bedsheets as if you are lost

Try to be some version of a perfect wife
Fuck like you are riding shafts of ice

The Cursing Psalm

O God! Have mercy on me, this clusterfuck.
Was there ever a time you were listening? Send me
some angels, mighty and ravening, sickled feathers

reaping o'er my head. Let's talk about vengeance
being mine. I have kept a list of grievances,
like scrolled-up parchments in my brain. Yea,

I cannot be rid of poisons. My grudges smell like arsenic.
Sniffing them bitters my mind. Some might say *forget!*
Not so easy for someone who floats her gripes

in formaldehyde – ugly, buckled things they are,
my specimens. It is hard not to open them, every now and then,
breathe in all the hurts. Have mercy on me come dusk –

hear me spelling myself to Hell with incant yowling,
hear me through the clingy vile of night. See thou in the dark,
grist thy teeth, gnaw the goodness out thy tongue –

set yourself to a mirror, spin your peepers round,
stitch the ghost of sideways looks upon the needle
of your eyes. Be a gatherer of them at social occasions,

nurse the beast of paranoia as you work. Bash your book
of payback psalms, flicker the pages of this nurtured tome –
every so often flowers, pressed thinly into a page.

A devoted nose can strain them for scents of ache.
Dig yourself deep, find the crypt. It hoards the pieces
of your heart. Pray and flail at Heaven

with your loose-linked smile. Exalt in faithfulness
to the dead if you must. You will see where you have touched
your things. The marks you have scraped in the dust.

Hood

There is always a wolf.
I am not going to stick to the path, not
when there is mystery in the wood. Not
when I see such flowers. I will sing
to their gathering, snap the stem beneath
the most beautiful heads. My grandmother
might find comfort in a memory of meadows.
On my arm, the basket swings like a wicker crib
with its brittle baby of wine and cake.
In the dark of the boles I hear breath. It clouds
from the gloom of a throat. It smells of gore
and gouging. Here I am, gaudy in the forest,
a bloom of blood. Here is my unexpecting flesh.
I see a window sick with tallow light,
the murder-shadow puppet of a beast
upon the pane. I should not have gone in
but I was captured by his growl of song,
lost my skin to the roughness of his tongue.
Stick to the way you know, my mother said.
Inside the forest are bones.

There are things that give me away if you know how to look,

that will help you crack my body's occult code. You might
get to know me well enough to learn my transmundane sight.
You might be aware of my smile, wide and radiant with teeth,
lips hauled back, cheeks bulbed into blush apples.
You might assume that my hair is the sun. You might be able to tell
that I cut my own fringe with weekly intensity, that I cannot
achieve a straight line, that I am aware of the feel of its growing
too near to my brows, of its creeping down my forehead like beetles
and slime. If you are behind me, you might try to stroke it.
Sometimes you have ruffled it as if I was a small child and you
left the idea of menace on my head. If you are reading this
and you are the one who once leaned in to smell it,
let me tell you that your breath was pure horror upon my neck.
You might tell me I look completely normal, that there is nothing
wrong, that there are no *usual* signs. You might have told me that I was
obviously in need of medical help / you might have made me feel
that I am one BIG FAT LIAR. The more I learn about myself,
the more I see the bad things I have done, or have said. Let me
tell you how much that makes me ~~hate~~ myself / ~~harm~~ myself
and the idea that you might find out makes me want to —
myself, sometimes. ~~Cross myself out~~. I am easily led. If you touched
me because it was easy / because I do not know how else to be loved /
because I wish I was lovely / because I was lonely / because between
right and wrong are nebulous lines / because you could, then
fuckyoufuckyoufuckyoufuck. I might misinterpret your friendship
and make you my moon and my stars. You might / love me
because I have smiled, wide and radiant with teeth for 49 years /
see all my rage / tell me it's okay / to be mad /
to un-hook my beam / break my face with a frown.

Frances Cornford's poem about a lady in gloves makes me realise that I have feelings for a woman for the first time

I make her a ten-fingered treasure of creamy vintage gloves.
Their softness elevates my shovel bones. I wear them
so she won't see my soiled, work-cracked hands. I think of her

and feel beautiful. Swank to the station, skirt flamed,
petticoat whispering. Under here I have trees – a crown
of leaves at the cusp of my two stout trunks. All this so I can sit

in second class, thinking *fuck you, Frances.* You
and your assumptions. I see no ladies, fatting through the fields –
just lawns and sheep, horse and copse, hedge and home,

cow and cold and my indelicacy, studded with magpie brooches,
big feet primly tucked. I wish I could peel back the years.
I am too old for such confusion, yet I muse upon her thumbs.

I follow goslings along the river path. Cannot take them home
no matter how the breeze saddens upon on their necks.
It's not my fault they're cold. I let them be, don't want to meet her

livid with the guilt of stolen geese. I see her length flick
its whipcord against the sky. I should have brought the silence
of my feral days, been subtle instead of damming the cobbles

with garrulous weight. I see her nape, her figments of knucklebone,
her hair. As dusk swapped its dilute for dark, I walked from the room
and I could not tell if her eyes had burned a butterfly

onto my back. My heels broke the soul of the stones.
I carried nothing upon my mouth but my own cold skin.
Tomorrow, I will crouch, knees apart in the soil.

Against the delphiniums, I will smell my pungent self.
The garden is where I waste my tenderness. As I fold the gloves
I think *next time, I'll just wear jeans. I love that you are so tall.*

The nights in which I fantasise an evensong of us

I opened my eyes and broke against a bland dawn,
imagined my burying against your body's smooth calf,
fancied your hand on my body's crypt in the shape of an epitaph.
We sang away the dark, woke to wash each other kitten clean,

lipped ourselves lush, softened our tongues with kinky psalms,
met in a chapel of scented sheets. I woke and lay like glass upon
the bruise of the bed, propped up like a relict, wore my flesh
in tones of mausoleum grey. This is a frequent sin – by noon

the guilt will settle the room like an weighty prayer, carry
its phantom on through the rest of the house. I predict I will lose
something important – a single glove or bunch of keys. I will pile
plates like communion discs, fold shrouds of vacant clothes.

The potatoes have come to a brutal end.
Scraped of a last comfort of soil and flayed raw,
I crisp the knife into their martyred starch, blunt their pale curves.
Their whittled skin settles the water like filthy floes.

It is necessary to carry on with these humdrum tasks.
I could bear it if I knew that you had thought of me today, even
in a fugitive moment. Midnight yields to the flame of our heads –
we melt like wax in the dark, make illuminations of ourselves.

Are Vaginas a Deal-Breaker Thing?

Let's face it. I am discomfited by my own, unsure
of the marsh, unsettled by its sodden pocket.
Use a mirror and get to know yourself, I once read
but I never got round to doing *that*.

I can imagine a world of moulded dolls, imagine simple acts
like brushing each other's hair, shopping for mushrooms.
We could build our chaste cairns upon the grass –
I'll tell you that your laugh is like a castle's wall

and you might say, *today is all about discovering.*
Might knock upon the bathroom door and see how my body
has shaped you the Orkneys. Tits like Egilsay and Wyre,
belly an Eynhallow – all stilling womb, all abandon.

All offer to birds. Or, you might say *scooch!* so we can spire
at opposite ends of the tub. I would use my best Joyce Grenfell voice
to tell you there really *is* a place there called Twatt.
I can think about lips, wrists, arms, neck – even take my eyes

all the way to your waist. Here is an offer of terrified flesh.
Here is where I speak politely of weather – we might touch
and I will swear you smell like snow, or earth or malt.
We might break against each other, squall and salt.

We could live in a cwtch of castles. I'll grow my hair

way on past my knees. Throw hanks of it out the split
of window when, like a dog, I sense the coming of your car.
Get me from this turret. I know how many stair rods
are swallowed by a smile. Our home would be built
from stones the shape of cherries. Licks of mortar
the colour of kirsch. You might find me one morning,
curled on the end of your bed like a cat.
My mouth is a lemon. Christ on a bike,
how will it be? I died inside a marriage – I said YES
to a holy cell and now I lock my life to the pledge
of my throat. I'm singing! Aye, when I think
of scurrilous things. Think of us, tipped and tingling.
No. Do you know, when he and I were courting, I wore
a necklace with his name spelled out in lead?
Trim the stairs with your enthusiasm. Every squeak
is the bleat of a sheep. I am the somewhere sound
of horses running wild. My face is a tilt of burning bricks.
Here I am, milky as a tamed cow, blousy as a hen.
Our home would be a marvel of medieval things.
I could talk you a tapestry, weave a wall of unicorns
right in front of our heads.

The First Time I Really, Properly Swim

Breathe and timid, walk – fiddle-foot a scree
of greasy rock. I did intend, in shorts to go
(maybe) up to the knee. There are strange words
upon the coal-Tyne's tongue. She's a babble
of gems, a belly of undercurrent. *I could bear you,*
I could flood your lungs. I am a vein of fish.
Never trust someone who can wear the sun
and still stay wet, I secretly think. Be wary
of someone who sucks the face off the moon.
Yet, the day is balm – layers of heat, a mild wind.
Look at my out-spanned crucifixion, shadow spread
along the shimmered hymn. My body brims with wants –
to wear the water's shroud, silver my bulge,
slip my hulk, re-write myself in rippled ink.
Easy does it. Slow and place each step on unseen bed,
swamp each calloused knee, christen goosey thighs.
I'm drowning the sag of my arse-cheeks, feel
the cold seep between my legs, wince as my vulva
is cupped by a curious hand. There's a silence
to being this far out, like you timewarped, slid
through the fabric of space, drifted to this bubble
of faraway sound. There's a fear of losing the shore.
Something bumps my leg – *Cthulhu!* This, in an age
is the most adventure I've had. It's washing me
young again (look at my grin), lifting me light as a leaf.
I take a little into my mouth – bitter iron, a thick tang
of oil and rust. From here, a full-on view of the little beach,
bound in a secret of canted trees.

I was not the eye of the Hubble. I saw no cosmic string.

Above, I see a watered night from all these fathoms down.
I have given up this falsity of bobbing, make a swallowed angel –
wing my shape into the seabed as I pray, heave the sea into my lungs

and lie there prone and psalming, eyes up to the overhead throb
and pulse. The jellyfish shiver their lights through invisible skin.
How alike they are to stars, with their trails of drowned light,

galaxies upon their soft-glass skin. I tell them gargled sermons,
bubble my litany of nonsensical things. *Oh pain, oh pain, oh pain,
oh pain.* I was born and will die to hymns of unrequited love.

Everyone seems to move on but me. An algae boulder, I'm stuck.
I am no astronaut – I floated once but only because of my breath.
Gravity has robbed me of planets. Here in the deep there will be

no claiming with flags, no one small step. I am no universe,
not even dust. I pretended Saturn's rings around my old home.
Wrote my days round – couldn't stick to the year's ecliptic.

Broke the circle of sun. Slipped the orbit, went off-kilter, was not
my satellite cushions, not my needlework, though the hoops were a study
of embroidered constellations. *Stop the thrashing, this pointless tread.*

*Give yourself up to the silky-cold embalming of yourself.
Be the sunken wreck.* I was not the wormhole of my mouth,
though its endless pit has eaten galaxies, swallowed junk.

I was not my cutlery drawer, though it was filled with sharps
and moons. I was a fool until I saw the ocean, felt salt and sand grit
against my shame. Clouds have now become a pod of whales.

The more I waded in, the lighter I became.

Villanelle to Cold Psalms

Here among the gloam owls, their cry of cold psalms
I am treetops, bearing a crown of night. The dark is born.
I imagine the death I would make in the strange of your arms,

shiver beneath the void of stars, sing the charm
of moths. Wish them against my neck. My skin mourns,
here among the gloam owls, their cry of cold psalms.

Dusk is a lie. This is crushed light, visions of curious calm.
I am prey, twitching in uneasy sleep, a distant spire's thorn.
I imagine the death I would make in the strange of your arms.

Here are the tendons of my neck. Here is the throb of harm.
I am lost as one drop of rain is lost to a storm,
here among the gloam owls, their cry of cold psalms.

I bear a ghost of gloom in the curl of my palm.
I am the moonlight's gash where the sky is torn.
I imagine the death I would make in the strange of your arms,

shiver of mist upon my mouth. I drink its balm,
damp upon the tip of thirst. Leave me to mourn,
here among the gloam owls, their cry of cold psalms.
I imagine the death I would make in the strange of your arms.

Quiero saber si tú aun me quieres and imagining seeing a bird burning in the sky

The sun is a blister. A sparrow aims the hunger
of her umber speck too high, is burned to a crisp for her pains.
There is barely any ash from her tiny gem of flight –
I catch what I can on my sympathetic tongue,
touch her soul to the back of my throat,

taste the misery of her scalded wings.
I heard her cry before she made a candle of herself –
saw the colours of her song, so much brighter
than her Earthen body was. I hear the efforts of my own heart,
wrangling with ideas of life inside the egg of my chest.

I cobble up a brew, though when I swill the milk
it sours, spoils the coffee's skin with curdled snow.
The radio spins me *Begin the Beguine. Y seguro yo estaba
que tú aun me querias.* The cup winks a foul brew that drools
from the handle of the spoon. I mop the floor and walk upon the spill.

I do not sink and it is like miracles. There were devils
and I have washed them away. The house is full of praise.
*You've been very good today. All the mess is ordered apple-pie –
you have made a soothing penance of the dust.* I have washed away
the cattywampus that my own body makes inside clothes.

Nobody could say that I'm not pulling my weight.
The family's empty skins are suffered to the line. I killed
their wet weight with plastic pegs. The wind breaks on flanks
of wool, makes each sock a goblet of air, stings around my knickers,
bloats each crotch. Dusk is too long in coming –

I must parade in full view, my sins entirely visible to the light.
Y hoy al verme tan solo sin ti. The sun will only set
when I have done with singing you in-between the lines.
Quiero saber si todo se olvida.
When I have done with such forbidden things.

Note:

The poem uses the version of *Begin the Beguine,* originally written by Cole Porter, as sung by Julio Iglesias.

Quiero saber si tú aun me quieres I want to know if you still want me
Y seguro yo estaba que tú aun me querias And I was so sure that you still loved me
Y hoy al verme tan solo sin ti Today, finding myself all alone without you
Quiero saber si todo se olvida I want to know if everything is forgotten

Study of Life as Recorded in Cruel Lines

I have gone into the waste lonely places/behind the eye; the lost acres
– From 'Meditations of an Old Woman (Part 4)' by Theodore Roethke

I have a new bad day, to add to the
    Great and Growing List Of Bad Days.
So far I have scratched about 17,000 marks (give or take) on the wall
of my skull. They tally each one of the days that I have passed
inside this shell (I do not count the baby years when I was just
a fat, pink bag of a thing who couldn't write and didn't spell).
When I am dead and they crack me open for science, for the
    Great Study Of This Massive Corybantic Nut
they will say *this creature had a head of infinitely repeated symbols.*
She wrote the passing of time in cruel lines –
she is interesting to Us because each of these lines
(when put under the microscope) is a hieroglyph.
They will crack the code of the one I wrote today –
discover that when my husband tried to get into bed with me
I screamed. Jumped up and made a huge fuss,
stamped my foot like a brat because I had everything arranged
and he made it un-arranged and I said *where?*
Where am I supposed to go if you're in here? Please.
He left with eyes like fly holes in fruit,
like the worst bruise on the best peach, like a broken bowl.
This will be listed inside his mind as the
    Latest Time I Have Gone Proper Mad
I am always trying to force my skin to want to be touched
and yet I have let it be touched, once too often, too many times.
They will read of all the muses I made of beautiful faces
how I broke my horrible plum of a heart
over dreams I built upon relative strangers,
like the one who sat at her table alone with fawn-coloured hair,
like the one with the broad chest beneath her tabernacle shirt.
They will see the times I was used as a cave for punishments of spunk.
I will be a chasm of such discoveries.
They will solve my cathedral of scrapes.

Grin Both Ways

So the morning begins. The same wish settles on my mind –
the peace of birds. I wish for the paradigm of feathers,
the luck of flight. To be easy as a dog's dream, clean as snow.

Outside, I see a crow balanced on wire. I see a tired garden,
a washout sky, dull mud, muted brick, every colour
dulled by winter mist. How easily I have fitted myself

to this loneliness, this new age of hiding away.
I look at the pane of glass, severing me from the cold.
Breathe a patch of fog upon it, trace one unbroken circle –

two open eyes. Sweep on a grin. The simple face
looks in at me, out at the opposite world and grins both ways.
I have to start myself again from scratch, go back

through every strange intricacy of my life – unpick
the cockled seam of every hour of suffered school, touch
around the sore wound of everyone I ever knew.

I turn to where the kitchen is quiet. There's no-one to hurt you
on plain days like this. I don't have to sketch on a smile.
There is nobody here to recognise but me.

The love that Orca taught me while he grew

Once his foal's lungs were fitted to small air.
Now, his beamy chest balloons with each need for wind –
I worship at his belly's rise and fall, his plush cathedral

padded with breath. His heart is a slow clock.
When I first saw his herd crowning the curve of a hill,
I thought of jigsaw whales. I saw him, half of the sweetest face

barely peeping round his mother's rump, coat a scrubbing brush,
knees like knots in string. One little calf from a piebald pod –
Orca I called you, then and there. The last bones

to fuse in the skeleton of a horse are the vertabrae –
that strength and structure creep through years of growth.
I thought of him as a patient wall, layering bulk and brick,

hanging ounce by ounce the whole weight of himself from a span
of spine. There is something good in knowing that we might
never really be a finished work. In the beginning, he shied

from my strange hands. I put away the scald of rope and sat for hours
upon the grass, plucking green spires and catching him only in
the corner of my eye. In our eleventh year I have shown him

most everything about myself, have worn my worst clothes
in front of him, have unashamedly cried. Together, we have learned
the trick of standing still, my cheek to his sun-warmed back,

his house of a head pressed to the dot of my own. I think that he is
my truest friend. I trust my skin to his teeth. I trust him
with my strange mouth, my odd words, my bother of unwanted thoughts.

I pull the comb through his fountain tail. He tends my loneliness
as if it were an ordinary thing. Every year, the martins spit their nest
on his stable wall. We watch them live a different life, high above

the routine of our own. I offer his mobile tongue my open palms,
kiss the slab of his brow, trace his irregular blaze as it falls like a wander
of snow. My four-square wonder keeps his hooves to the roots.

We have an understanding with the ground.

Ode to the Sight of my Coloured Cob

O! The best days are the ones when the acres slip, easy as miracles
under my feet – where the mead is a green heaven, where buttercups serve
just as well for constellations. I never got used to having a horse –
like maybe one day, to check if I'm really awake, I will tweak my arm
and pinch the luck of him away. Maybe, when I stretch the joy
of his two-beat name, sing its opera to the wide land, I'll find that he

was a fancy I tried to make real with flesh. Or maybe he's foundered down,
broken-backed, or dead with one malicious crow fettered to his brow
like a bad crown and I think *this is too good a thing, too good a thing
for the likes of you.* But then I make it to the scrubby cusp, look down
and *there.* O! My heart turns cock-a-hoop – the sky opens blue
above him like a lazy smile. There he is, pastern-deep in the socket of bog

that he loves no matter how I wish he would keep away, muzzle dipped
to the herbs. From here I can see he is not lame, not warped by colic,
not cut. My heart swells like autumn's fruit. I see the ghosts from where
he has rolled away his winter hair. O! if they would rise – make him
many times again that I could love them all, offer my honest palms
as leaves of adulation to every lip. He sees me – crimps the sockets

round each brindle eye and shakes the settled drowse from his scow
of a head, like coming to after you had the most refreshing sleep.
He tucks my voice into his somnolent ears, flicks the shamble of hair
along his mast of a neck and casts away, blunt cask of breast prowing
the swell of grass like the slow ship that he is. He comes to me with
the weight of mountains kept beneath his skin. Comes to me mild as dust.

The gifts she got at birth

When she was born, they gave her Good / Fairy / Bad / Fairy gifts.
Leaning over her rhythmic crib, they bestowed their spoil in gabbles above
the unsuspecting child. *Be graceful,* they bade her.
Be beautiful, witty and good.

Bad / Fairy said *you will die, You will die, and all your dreams*
will be filled with spikes and wheels.

She did not manage to grow in an elegant way.
Elephant legs and pup-fat plump, sitting in class with her head
switched off, much afraid of fractions, worried sick on nouns.

Before she turned Sweet Sixteen, she had been
punched in the head for carrying a yellow lunchbox
slapped in the face for wanting to ride on a swing
humiliated for making funny noises in school
fingered because she did not know why it was wrong
sent out to play when she had no friends
smacked with hands / slippers for being bad
called ugly / weird at least three times a week
told that she was an accident by her mum

She began her century of sleep and feared the interference of a man.
This would be no way to wake, a pair of unfamiliar lips pressing
to her own, as if they would steal her breath.

She was insulated by a wall of thorns, as hard to get in as get out.

The stones wept with dreams. The castle was kept so still.

Poor blackbird crumb

It flew into the window *bang* poor thing and fell
to the ground like a dreadful leaf poor blackbird mote so warm

  and me so big we threw our house in front of its flight
it broke upon fraudulent glass this is how we close ourselves

off from the world and still think we see everything
come make your not-dead not-dead ascension

  I said   *so warm and soft*   still It's alive *it's alive*
I believed just stunned just   all the wind knocked out

of its divine breast   the luck gone from under its wings
I tried to barter the price of its spark for the weight of my head

 a small expense one beautiful life for this blown shell
so that it might rise like a knife through the blue skin above

I held it close poor blackbird tomb craw to throat
so light I think it might be the same weight   as my own heart

  It did not move where was its air?   where was its tilt?
poor blackbird crumb   so perfectly made for sky

I cannot lie down so quickly   and be done I am glad it will
only hurt today and not   tomorrow again   again

  a doomish milk ruined its beady sight blunted the keen
of its yellow-bezel eye my palm became a gentle church

I made a charm to wake a life *dawn-break*
sing-mist feather-magic   weather-sigh hop-toe babble-bright

  I tried to voice the flowing   back to halted blood
I tried   to make it cry back alive

Be subtle as the Snow Queen,

blank as the skim of her sleigh's cold pass.
Be skinned as a haunted mirror, raw with light,
a splinter that sings as they cry your scratches out.
Turn soft to stone, wind back time and crack your weight
to a moon-drowned slab. Suffer the lion who reeks of God
or seek for lamps to throw yourself against. Adore the fold
of oversize coats. Be giddy on goat-shaped legs.

Be the unattainable ring. Spock your ears and faff your throat
with brooches, m*ore Galadriel than Gollum,*
if you can, dear. Stop this fingering of squabbled gold.
Speak in portents, wear your hair like water to your waist.
Bind the dark. Catch an apocalyptic horse and spiel it soothed.
Baffle with unknown tongues. Be the catastrophe of mountains.
Crave to be un-wrought. Offer your gimcrack to flames.

The truth began with a mirror, cruel and clean

It had been too easy to see themselves as angels   too easy
to button collars up tight across their throats   too easy to keep
each avid pulse hidden beneath their skin   Once   there might
have been a time when the world was purely good
but the mirror had been carried Heaven-ways up

abused the sky inside its one great noxious eye
turned the blue to canker   switched clouds to calamity
It warped the beauty of birds in its one malevolent blink   laughed
itself into the shape of splinters   shivered into showers
settled its bitter dust upon the Earth   Once

there were children and they loved to talk   to play   to tend
their flowers   each other very much   Once   the boy thought
he saw the swirling flakes make the shape of a woman
fearsome keen   She peered through the little   leaden
diamond panes and numbed his soul with her gaze

of flint   of un-settlement   of snowy silent death   Once
they grew roses   frost had bitten all the rosebuds   burned
them dim   The petals fell like charred rain   drifted the path below
like old blood   He learned the squinted pain of spoiled sight
looked upon her ruined flesh   felt the glass go slanted in his heart

Magic Mirror

I am stilled water   I am polished stone
a fatted drop of blood   I have given your faces
back to you   since you first learned to look
at yourselves   in the side of a polished cup
in a puddle a window pane   in the toe
of a patent shoe I am the splinters   of dropped glass
slipped from a devil's hands   I am a splinter
in the eye split-blink ice-knife   see yourself
and sob out tears of snow   Who is the fairest
who is the fairest   *Mirror, mirror* Wicked
Stepmother asked me this   and I said *hey, yeah,*
you of course. Who else   Not model symmetry
orthodontic straight line   pearly no blemish
Barbie bullshit no   Hazel flecks on an iris
get me thinking   *Fiver, silflay, Frith* You see frizz
I see hay in a horse field   escaped orts uneaten
thick locks bladder wrack   Short hair thistlefuzz.
barley rust raven's wing ash   Brows owl plume
Whiskers a stubble field   your chin a crop
of stalks I see a harvest   You are evolution you
are mass of seasons   your birth your youth
your age your death To start   bald in a marshmallow's skin
grow to an end rinded in bark   Think of me as
as an iridescent pit   a speculum on a bird's wing
Kay cannot recall when the world   was wonderful
Gerda is monstrous   roses are skew
He will search for the Queen   with her cape of dead pelts
Beauty will scrute for the Beast   see its heartbreak
I'll show you your soul if you have one   deal crystal atoms of luck
At night my oval is dead   with half-seen things
car lamp flash   crack in the hallway door
Minnows   of momentary light

My Offering to the Earth

Time is passing. A garden grieves beneath a weight
of temporary death, yet it can bear this null sleep.
Breaking buds show bloom is almost due.
Thyme is making tiny leaves – my fingers lightly press
its scent. Toes cold from the wet ground,
nails bunged with mud, I'll tell you how hopeful I was
when I walked down the aisle, all fluff,
all vision of cakes, dews of pearl on each veiled ear.
The organ's hoarse groan marched my foamy progress.
My hair was stiff with spray and grips.
The Best Man painted HE LP on the soles
of my husband's shoes so that when he knelt,
the congregation tittered about impending doom.
Spring is turning the bare ground, sprigging a naked tree
that has stood, raking the dark like the rack of a rutting hart.
Rain studs the kiss of a leaf.
The evening stiffens over what I have grown.
I pluck at weeds, smooth the holes they leave,
watch the roosting birds.

November's Spoil of Rain and Plague

I am the daughter of stopped clocks – those plastic moons
where moments have stuck. Too late for elevenses,
much too soon for lunch. I am the halting of time,
its unwound tether of hands, the slicing of dials.

I am Sunday's child though I am not blithe, or bonny.
Wise nor good. My stars are not aligned, I am not cusped.
I am a mother's failed prediction. How massive my love can be,
how my tongue lolls like a dog, how I wear my heart

like a pelt of brindle screams! Come to the crush
of my great arms – I am Kraken, the page you wrote
in the Burn Book. Edward's fingered knives.
I am cupboards on uncertain afternoons –

the cube of petrified OXO, the sadly chipped cups.
Allow me to offer my stains. I have held you in my brain
and failed to shift your face. Fur and carcass –
something ate the heart of me and wasted the rest.

My mother was a tunnel and I slithered from her,
wet and helpless, squawking, gross. They broke
the length of ferrous wire between us, belly to blood.
It fed me on ash and blades, on something I can still taste.

Ways in which I came to be a thief

I stole the worship of birds like a jealous priest
counted their songs into a miser's hoard
lay like a slab beneath their flight
plucked the ground of feathers the shape of knives

I stole the view of lurching pines
and filled my sight with spears
saw them flinch against the harrowing wind
and tack their needles to pale air

I stole the kitchen's robe of dismal breath
so I could pity the schism of one dropped cup
and cry for soap clung to spoons like throttled cum
and taste light served upon the brittle wheel of plates

I stole my mother's history of bones
carried the weight of her loury face
suffered my eyes to the wraith of her gaze
hooded her ghost with the mimic of her own frayed lids

I stole the mirror's fear
when I broke upon its bevelled edge
blinked away her caustic green
opened my own shade of sky

The Altar of the Dead

Strew it with leaves,
       with fronds, with flowers.   Watch
   the petals slowly bruise.   Smell
the ruined beauty,   see the petals stain
with despair.   This is the window,
the   slot where they say you can bring them
           back. For a while,   they might
awake.

Make a shrine of a photograph.   Pray
to the curve of a lover's neck,
wear the weal of their smile again, just like
    the first time you suffered beneath its fascinating slash.
Here is the snapshot of its scythe.   Rasp your recollections
sharp afresh, squint along its edge.
Wish away the years,   before you wore too many of them,
heavier each time upon your skin.

   Ask
the plastic saints to wake the arms of a ghost.
   Ask
the pinioned Christ to free them from the relic of your heart.
   Ask
the curls of incense to bring them here again.

Spun from the Same

I see a history of us, as our reflections pool the window
of the train. Pasture reels – slipstreams of forest sing
to our twin faces. My son, the apple that didn't fall

far from the tree. I see the mirror of our substantial bone,
the family nose. My fingers are fixed to my child's hands.
We bite at hangnails just the same, as blinks of sheep

and flickers of cow flash past. Look at the dots of outside light
that land in our eyes just the same – same chin, same cheeks,
same way of thrilling with excitements at our little trip,

this brave adventure, on our own. Our secret grins are wide
as distant hills, are spun from the same mouth. Each time
I fix my gaze, I see something new. He spools these long legs,

fidgets at the confine of the carriage seat – I dangle
dumpy trunks, wonder how I gave him such height. Maybe
in some other life I'm a telegraph pole, a tree, a tower

and he's from this other magic. Right now, we're travelling
the same track. The land spreads like quick cloth. Each minute,
a new horizon – lines cut through us, each scene a sever.

We snack on crisps. The glass spangles with birds. How much
will I be guilty, later on? I tell myself you cannot inherit a brain.
How much will he keep? How much did I already break?

The Un-flight of Porcelain Birds

My pretty flock, my throng of bisque,
brittle murmuration, flinty perched.
Silent wards of song, dawn finds you unyielding –
no rising in your tinted eyes.
If you drop, you fail to fly.
Your breasts crack. Your little heads shatter,
make the floor a nest of spelks,
a splint of muted beaks.
Spillikins of feather,
your wings are kept by clay.
Roost in my palm, echo of wild things.
You have never trembled evening from your throat.
You have never known
the blue sail of sky.

How the river takes whatever you pray

  I heard a faraway chapel of birds
pure as the call of distant Sunday bells
   They flew above the liquid's supple tongue
  as it rolled a wet hymn across feral land
I must answer the call of this cordial font
dip some part of my own self in   unwhole to be made
whole   Every path   every twist   every road   everywhere
  I place my feet seems like a pilgrimage
   I'm walking to see if there is a heaven somewhere
   I was planted and then I was ripped up
   by the root   I lost my place on the soil
   and now I remember how I used to meet
   the lapping edge to swim   I try to find
  the place where I used to venture down
 looked for relics of my tread but winter had already been
  and spring has moved its newly living way
    and the overwhelming flood had changed
     the landscape of the banks   There was no record
    here that I had ever passed
   I saw the grey priest of a heron
fly overhead like a slow angel   bearing the crucifixion
of its splinter feet   I came here for a cure
but I cannot smooth my terror down   my skin is blistered
with odd tones   curves with cold   My mind carries you softly
just like the water bears the mild burden of ruined leaves
  I kneel to sink my hand into epiphanies
   I see you   I hear you   I know that you are there
    I love you   I love you
     wherever you have gone
      I sent you a drowning prayer
       I saw the river and cried

If we are here when yellow has done with the year

Yellow is the colour of dread.
I see the acres drown.

Yellow is the colour of smothering –
I see the crop's raw ocean

spin the horizon gold, break its flood
against the yonder paddock fence

where a chestnut horse walks beneath the sun
like a bonfire of muscle and hot, bright skin.

Dandelions are the colour of life.
I see them haze with bees,

weigh with tomorrow's honey.
Days travel quick around their gaudy clocks,

for yellow is the colour of passing time.
Their faces will turn to snow.

Is Autism/Covid happening to someone/somewhere else?

I told the counsellor that I had been okay,
when she asked how I had been. Good, even.
The roads are so quiet. On my walks, I haven't seen a soul.
I function well in this new confine. *Do autistic people
feel guilty?* I go to the laptop and look myself up,
like (over this last year) I have learned to do.
It's there (I think), buried beneath a few mute layers
like a pea through a mattress. I told the counsellor *I am the happiest
I have been for a long while. Is this bad?* I go to the laptop

and use the statistics to try and make it real. It's real (I think)
and when I read the fear of my Facebook friends, I realise that I am unhinged,
am without gravity, am floating away. I smack my palm to my head,
try to thump it in. I feel as if I was built to thrive inside
these new, restricted days. My son cannot go anywhere
and this has taken all the murder/road wreck/violent fears away.
I told the counsellor that I am using predictive text more and more,
to help me show that I care. *I am so sorry. I love you.*
It keeps me looking human, in everyone else's sight.

A hedgehog fell into my neighbour's water bucket during the night,
though we try to be good and catch these precious pools,
try to learn not to squander the gift of useful rain.
The hedgehog sank and it became too much death, much too near.
I thought about the damp skin that closed above its head,
how it saw the dusk through a quivering window,
how it opened its mouth to the shape of the moon.
How the water stole away its tiny breath,
how its spines held a hostage of dew.

I thought about its bed of cold flood, its doused eyes,
its final small and smothering room. It was meant to keep on
crossing the dark road, shadowing the way with its plump wedge,
meant to keep on tramping down its boundaries,
wearing its routes into the eternally familiar. If it can die like this,
then the usual owls might drown in the evening sky,
the bats could fall from the twilight like sad rain –
the trees will end up failing to wear the stars upon their brittle heads.
There will be no more predictability of things.

The Advent Calendar of Most Useful Things

Behind door no. 1 A stranger's smile cut from a magazine
Behind door no. 2 The feeling of approaching rain
Behind door no. 3 A healthy mushroom dome
Behind door no. 4 A bradawl's point
Behind door no. 5 Broth mix
Behind door no. 6 Some obsolete currency
Behind door no. 7 A tawny owl's incantation
Behind door no. 8 Your favourite carol sung tuneless and loud
Behind door no. 9 A lucky horseshoe
Behind door no. 10 An atlas of made-up lands
Behind door no. 11 Permission slip for a pantomime
Behind door no. 12 One outlandish moustache
Behind door no. 13 Two slices of wholemeal toast
Behind door no. 14 A dish of trifle with no calories
Behind door no. 15 A squished *Chapstick* stuck with pocket lint
Behind door no. 16 Empty (to encourage Seasonal Perplexity)
Behind door no. 17 A genuine vintage *Babycham* glass (with deer)
Behind door no. 18 Your child's first tooth
Behind door no. 19 A unicorn made from driftwood
Behind door no. 20 A matchbox full of seaglass from the beach
Behind door no. 21 A stout shoe
Behind door no. 22 The brackish taste of an icicle
Behind door no. 23 A friend's name from your past
Behind door no. 24 The smell of a blown-out candle
Behind door no. 25 An Arctic hare in the shape of your mind

If Ω Is For The Last Thing I Might Ever Do

I could find myself an altar of grass   lay in the shape of an offering
patibulum of arms outstretched   under a host of birds
Let the sunlight   make a crux gemmata of my plain skin
crypt the air   with quietus breath

thinking *this   This is eternity, my friends* Ω

Or I could swing from the kitchen doorway like a rood   and let
my family pass beneath my intersect   like pilgrims
I could ward this sanctuary   with the anger of punished wood
This room is a tabernacle   an ambry of bone-pale bread

thinking *if this has to be the end   at least you have been fed* Ω

Acknowledgements

'How Austistic Spectrum Condition Made Her Worth Her Weight in Birds' won 2nd prize in the 2020 *Sentinel Literary Quarterly* poetry competition (published in a slightly different form). 'Mrs/Mother Hail' was highly commended in the 2021 Red Shed poetry competition. 'Self-Portrait as an Inferno' first published on *Idle Ink*. 'Fairy Stories' first published in the *Twice Upon a Time* anthology, Kind of a Hurricane Press. 'Fat Alice' first published on *Ink, Sweat & Tears*. 'This is a Frankenstein Night' first published on *Fragmented Voices*. 'Red' first published in *14 Magazine*, Vanguard Editions. 'Frances Cornford's poem about a lady in gloves makes me realise that I have feelings for a woman for the first time' first published (in a slightly different form) in *Warriors, Witches, Workers*, Culture Matters. 'Are Vaginas a Deal-Breaker Thing?' first published on *Poethead*. 'We could live in a cwtch of castles. I'll grow my hair' first published (in a slightly different form) in *Domestic Cherry*. 'The First Time I Really, Properly Swim' shortlisted in the 2019 *Grindstone Literary* poetry competition. 'Villanelle to Cold Psalms' first published on *Poethead*. 'Look at me, lingering outside this murdered church' first published in *Strix*. 'Poor blackbird crumb' shortlisted for the Bridport Prize, 2021. 'The truth began with a mirror, clean and cruel', 'Study of Life as Recorded in Cruel Lines' and 'Schneewittchen and the Universe' all first published in *The Rialto*. 'Magic Mirror' first published in anthology, *White Noise & Ouija Boards, Three Drops from a Cauldron*. 'November's Spoil of Rain and Plague' first published on *Poethead*. 'Spun from the Same' commended in the 2018 *Mother's Milk* poetry competition. 'The Un-Flight of Porcelain Birds' first published on *Poethead*. 'Is Autism/COVID happening to someone/somewhere else?' First published in the *100 Poems to Save the Earth* anthology, Seren, 2021. 'The Advent Calendar of Most Useful Things' first published on *Ink, Sweat & Tears*.